YOU CAN'T WEAR P[A]

Justine Avery

Kate Zhoidik

No. . . YOU can't wear panties!

I wear Big-Girl panties!

No. . . YOU can't wear panties!

I wear Big-Girl panties!

No. . . YOU can't wear panties!

I wear Big-Girl panties!

No... YOU can't wear panties!

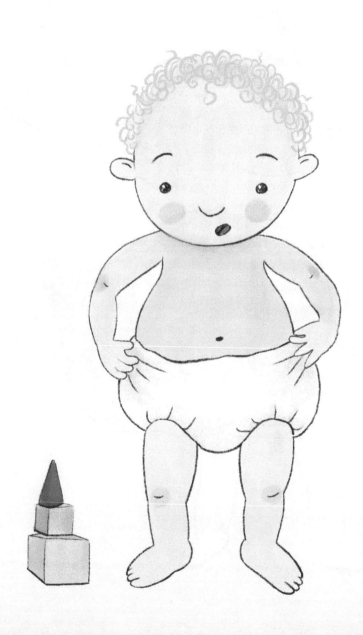

I wear Big-Girl panties!

No. . . YOU can't wear panties!

I wear Big-Girl panties!

No. . . YOU can't wear panties!

I wear Big-Girl panties!

No... YOU can't wear panties!

I wear Big-Girl panties!

No. . . YOU can't wear panties!

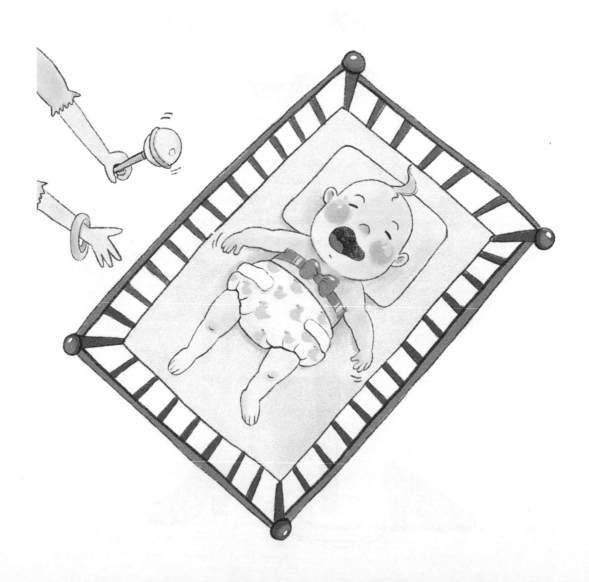

I wear Big-Girl panties!

No. . . YOU can't wear panties!

I wear Big-Girl panties!

No. . . YOU can't wear panties!

I wear Big-Girl panties!

No. . . YOU can't wear panties!

I wear Big-Girl panties!

For the proudest
big girl of them all,
you never cease
to amaze and delight us.
—J.A.

To my granny
who gave me
a fabulous childhood.
—K.Z.

Justine Avery is an award-winning author who loves writing stories for all sorts of readers. She was born in America but grew up—and is still growing up—all over the world as a natural explorer with a curiosity for all things. She's jumped out of airplanes, off of very high bridges, and into shark-infested waters—to name a few adventures. And books are her favorite adventures of all.

Kate Zhoidik is from Serbia where she lives with her daughter and two guinea pigs. She likes to crochet toys and dance flamenco.

First published 2021 by Suteki Creative

FIRST EDITION

Copyright © 2021 Justine Avery
Illustrated by Kate Zhoidik
All rights reserved.

ISBN: 978-1-63882-219-6
ISBN: 978-1-63882-208-0 (ebook)
ISBN: 978-1-63882-207-3 (hardcover)
ISBN: 978-1-63882-039-0 (audio book)

Discover More...
uniquely wonderful, utterly imaginative children's books by Justine Avery.

Visit JustineAvery.com
and join in the exclusive
fun & freebies.

9 781638 822196